# A PORTFOLIO OF

# PORCH
# &
# PATIO
# IDEAS

# CONTENTS

© Copyright 1996
Cy DeCosse Incorporated
5900 Green Oak Drive
Minnetonka, Minnesota 55343
1-800-328-3895
All rights reserved

Library of Congress
Cataloging-in-Publication Data
A Portfolio of Porch & Patio Ideas
p. cm.

ISBN 0-86573-983-8 (softcover)
1. Porches—Design and construction. 2. Patios—Design and construction.
3. Porches—Designs and plans. 4. Patios—Designs and plans.
I. Cy DeCosse Incorporated. II. Series
TH4970.P687 1996
690'.184—dc20
95-49809 CIP

Author: Home How-To Institute™
Creative Director: William B. Jones
Associate Creative Director: Tim Himsel
Group Executive Editor: Paul Currie
Managing Editor: Carol Harvatin
Editors: Mark Biscan, Jon Simpson
Art Director: Geoffrey Kinsey
Copy Editor: Janice Cauley
Vice President of Development
    Planning & Production: Jim Bindas
Production Coordinator: Laura Hokkanen

Printed on American paper by Webcrafters Inc. (0496)

CY DECOSSE INCORPORATED

A COWLES MAGAZINES COMPANY

Chairman/CEO: Bruce Barnet
Chairman Emeritus: Cy DeCosse
President & Chief Operating Officer: Nino Tarantino
Editor-in-Chief: William B. Jones
99 98 97 96 / 5 4 3 2 1

# WHAT MAKES A GREAT PORCH OR PATIO?

Porches and patios are unique indoor/outdoor areas that link the interior of your home with the surrounding yard and landscape. More than a place to put umbrellas and wet boots, or than an empty slab of concrete in the back yard—porches and patios expand usable living spaces and provide a comfortable setting for a number of indoor and outdoor activities.

Porches have been a prominent feature of American homes since the arrival of the first settlers. Patios, on the other hand, have only been a part of the American outdoor scene since the end of World War II. Porches and patios satisfy our desire to feel a part of nature whenever possible by providing an outdoor environment — with interior comforts.

Porches capture the essence of earlier eras and small-town living. A newspaper landing with a thud on the porch in early morning signals the start of the new day; at night, the porch is a place for quiet reflection or romantic moments. Porches let in cooling breezes on hot summer days and provide a protected place for kids to play on a rainy afternoon. They add distinctive detail to any home and create a graceful transition between the open space of the outdoors and the enclosed structure of the house.

The vast selection of materials and design options makes patios one of the most functional and convenient ways to create an outdoor living area. Patios can be constructed from a number of attractive all-weather materials, such as brick or concrete, and built into almost any setting. Patios establish the foundation, or floor, of your outdoor room, providing solid, level footing for people, as well as outdoor furniture and planting containers.

*A Portfolio of Porch & Patio Ideas* is filled with colorful photos to inspire you with ideas and help you discover how a porch or patio can enhance your outdoor living, allow you to enjoy the fresh air from a protected setting and add an exciting appeal to any outdoor area.

**An all-season sun porch** *is a relatively new concept in porches that is becoming very popular, especially in regions where weather prohibits year-round outdoor activity.*

**A classic portico** *frames the front entry to this home. The small porch not only makes an attractive addition, it provides a sheltered space for those entering or exiting the house.*

4

*This beautiful brick patio* naturally brings together the functional areas of the home with the outdoors. Social gatherings and other indoor activities can expand outdoors onto the patio, yet remain linked with the interior of the house. The large potted plants link the patio with the natural surroundings outdoors.

Photo courtesy of Minneapolis Public Library, Minneapolis Collection William G. Wallof, photographer

*(right)* **Porches were essential** on Victorian houses built during the late 1800s. These elaborate designs were highly decorative and functional.

*(below)* **Early nineteenth century porches** were wide, with deep, overhanging eaves and decorative balustrades. Second-story porches were usually located off a bedroom to provide cool breezes in the summer. This particular home features second-story and third-story porches.

Photo courtesy of Minneapolis Public Library, Minneapolis Collection A.D. Roth, photographer

*Planning*
# THE HISTORY OF PORCHES & PATIOS

Porches and patios evolved from a desire for comfortable, functional outdoor living spaces. Porches were first imported from the Middle East to Greece, Spain, Italy and other European countries where they remain a part of the culture in one form or another. In the United States, porches were imported from France to the Deep South in the early 18th century. The elaborate wraparound and two-story porches still seen on Victorian-style houses throughout the South are a perfect example of porches designed at the height of their popularity.

Patios first originated in Spanish and Italian villas. They functioned as open-air courtyards, completely enclosed, in the middle of these structures. Patios became a part of the American landscape after World War II, when cheaper, easier-to-maintain materials became available and people started to utilize the valuable outdoor space in their backyards.

Patios are an evolution of the porch. Put a roof over an attached patio, and you have a porch. Up until this point, porches were the center of outdoor family life. They were a place to sit and watch what was going on in the front of the house. By the end of World War II, many homes were built without the traditional front porch; instead, they had small, raised platforms, called stoops, at the entrances to their homes. Most of the family outdoor activity began to take place in the backyard, which used to be considered primarily a children's play space.

Porches and patios are attractive, multifunctional features that will add personal and property value to any home. Although they are related, porches and patios are distinctly different, and each will interact in different ways with your house and surrounding yard. As you evaluate your site, think about the different ways a porch or patio will affect the existing setting.

*"To see and be seen" was one of the basic purposes of porches designed in the early 1900s. Large formal porches, such as the expansive veranda on the front of the house shown here, were an important part of the social communications of the times.*

7

*A **contemporary outdoor setting** features a poolside patio as well as a second-story veranda, with a small set-back porch tucked underneath.*

# THE HISTORY OF PORCHES & PATIOS

Porches have been a part of the American homestead since the earliest days of this country's existence. Originally intended as a shelter from sun and rain, porches also serve as a transitional area between the interior and exterior of the house. Only since the 1950s has the popularity of patios as versatile, outdoor multifunctional spaces increased.

After World War II, architectural elements that required timely and expensive upkeep were replaced by easier-to-maintain options, such as brick or asphalt patios. Many people eliminated their porch, or enclosed it and converted it to an interior room. With the exception of the South, the popularity of porches declined. Soon the backyard patio and barbecue were the center of family gatherings and the focal point for leisure-time activities.

New innovations in porches and patios reflect the growing interest in our outdoor living spaces. Porches and patios can be created to fit almost any specifications you desire, due to new ideas in porch and patio design and the new materials available today. These innovations reflect the growing interest in increasing the quality of our outdoor living area—outdoor rooms that function as an extension of the indoors to the outside.

The newest innovation in indoor/outdoor living spaces is the glass-enclosed porch, or sun porch. Similar to traditional conservatories, these rooms are built using energy-efficient materials, such as thermal glass, heat-absorbing tiles and climate-control technology. Originally designed to bring the sun's warmth into the home, they are popular in climates where weather prohibits year-round outdoor living.

**This elaborate two-story, wraparound porch** is typical of the Victorian-style porches found throughout the South. Before the invention of air-conditioning these outdoor living areas were the coolest places for families to gather and socialize.

**This contemporary sun porch,** completely enclosed by glass, creates the illusion of being in an outdoor setting, with the comfort and convenience of being indoors.

*This sunny patio* was designed with a low, open railing so users can enjoy as much of the beautiful scenery as possible, even when seated.

*Natural brick* makes a safe and attractive poolside surface. The rich red brick is used throughout the landscape, in retaining walls and as a border for planting areas, giving the entire setting a unified look.

## Planning

# DEFINE THE FUNCTION

Begin planning your porch or patio project by making a wish list specifying the possible functions of your porch or patio area. Focus on how this space will be used, not so much what it will look like. Think about your lifestyle, your family's lifestyle and the activities each member enjoys. Also consider how the different elements of your house and yard will integrate into one dynamic design. For example, how will a porch or patio affect the overall look of your home and surrounding landscape? Porches and patios should enhance the house, not overwhelm it. Other important issues to consider include: how private or public you want your porch or patio area to be, and the budget limitations you will face taking on such a project. Your budget will be a major factor in determining the features and materials you can include, and those you'll have to do without.

Porches can be used for a variety of functions: entertaining, dining, a children's play area, an outdoor sleeping space or restful reading area. Porches also have strictly practical purposes, such as protecting the front entry, providing shade for interior rooms and enjoyment of the outdoors in inclement weather. When building a porch, as part of a new home or as an addition to an existing one, think ahead about possible future uses for the space. If you build an open porch now, you may want to enclose it at some future date. Knowing and planning for this now can make future changes much easier.

Patios provide a sense of privacy without being confining. A good patio design will accommodate and adjust to your family's various activities, from quiet dinners to festive social gatherings. Patios become more flexible when they include features that are multifunctional, such as built-in benches that can be used for storage, or that double as low tables.

A porch or a patio can change the shape of the house, give it a better sense of scale and unify the overall look of the setting. It can add texture and shape to an outdoor environment, naturally extend interior spaces and enable you to enjoy more time outdoors.

**A modern sun porch** *expands the kitchen and creates an entire indoor living area, with the look and feel of the outdoors.*

**A cozy backyard porch** *offers a protected place to play on a rainy day. It's also a convenient way to keep an eye on the kids from indoors while they play outdoors.*

11

# Planning
# ASSESS THE SITE

What are the positive and negative aspects of your yard? Is there a view you wish to enjoy? Or a sunny exposure you want to take advantage of? Study the effects of the sun, shade and wind as they move across different areas of the yard. Also consider sources of noise and privacy needs of your site as it currently exists. Use this information when making decisions about the function, style, location and size of your proposed porch or patio.

Patios and porches on the north side of a house receive little sunlight, so they remain relatively cool, while those facing south are warmed by the sun for a good part of the day. Porches and patios facing east stay fairly cool because they only receive morning sunlight. Those located on the west side of a house will be quite warm because they receive the sun at its strongest, from midafternoon on. The southeast or southwest corner of a house receives the most comfortable balance of sunlight.

Porches and patios should take advantage of pleasant views. Think about the view, from every direction, as you determine the location of your porch or patio. The location also depends on the size of your lot, the way your house sits on it and the way you've planned to use the space.

Design your porch or patio in proportion to its intended use. A patio that is too large will lack a sense of enclosure. If your lot is large, consider a series of patios, rather than one large one, or a wraparound porch with different porch areas on separate sides of the house. The size and shape of the porch or patio should complement and be in scale with your house, as well as its intended use. Strategically placed patios and porches that wrap around the house are ways to make the most of sun and shade exposures as they change throughout the day.

(below) **This picturesque patio** area extends outward creating a connection between the indoor and outdoor living areas. Because of this connection a beautiful view becomes part of the backyard.

Photo courtesy of Bomanite Corp.

(above) **The sloping terrain of this backyard** required a unique design for this sunken patio. One side of the patio is a retaining wall that can be used for additional seating. The design not only makes an attractive addition to the backyard, it also make the yard much more functional.

**An overhead pergola** *offers a break from the hot sun as it scatters shadows across this sunny backyard patio. The grand stature and style of the pillars and pergola give the setting a formal feel.*

**Enclosing a portion of this outdoor deck** *with a screened porch creates another functional outdoor living space. The enclosed area is protected from the sun, as well as from insects and other outdoor pests.*

# PORCH MATERIALS

Porches can be incorporated into almost any home plan. The architectural design, types of materials and style of finishing detail influence the overall appeal of a porch. Architectural elements, such as decorative Victorian-style balusters and railings, add a sense of old-style elegance to a porch. Traditional house designs, such as midwestern farmhouse or western ranch-style, are the most common types of homes to which porches are added, although most contemporary-style homes can also accommodate a porch.

Traditionally, porches are made of wood or brick. Because they require continuous maintenance, wooden porches are often thought of as a "luxury" when it comes to designing a home. Developments in outdoor building materials have made a number of new options for porch construction available. These new materials are popular because they are more durable and virtually maintenance-free. They also offer innovative new ways to enhance the aesthetic appeal of a porch. One example is the use of more types of translucent materials, such as clear plastics, which enable people to build porches that bring more natural light into an interior space.

Whether you are adding a new porch to the front of your home or refurbishing an existing one, maintaining the architectural integrity and design style of the home is crucial to the successful integration of new and existing elements.

Photo courtesy of Walpole Woodworkers Inc.

***The classic charm of a porch*** *is enhanced by the traditional design of the finishing details. Turned spindles and colonial post caps beautifully complement the architectural design of the home.*

***A portico*** *frames the front of this home and captures the rustic look of the rest of the exterior.*

Photo courtesy of Cy DeCosse Inc.

*Ornamental cast stone* was used to replicate authentic detail, once captured in stone, in concrete. The neo-classic design of the columns, balustrades and railings coordinates with the Mediterranean-style design of the rest of the house.

*Common colors and materials* create a sun porch that blends beautifully with the rest of the exterior. The glassed-in porch brings the beauty of nature indoors. A sliding patio door eliminates the barrier between inside and out and creates a comfortable link between the two areas.

*The Old-World beauty of this classic front porch makes it an architectural highlight and the shining glory of this home.*

# Design
# PORCH OPTIONS

The concept of a porch brings specific images to mind. By definition, porches are exterior appendages with a roof and a floor, often built at an entrance to a house. Porches are referred to by a number of different names, such as porticos, verandas or piazzas, depending on the size and location of the structure. The various terms used to describe porch structures originated from a number of different sources: Italy, Spain and Greece, to name a few, and are often used interchangeably to describe the same structure. For example, a porch that spans the front of a house could be referred to as a porch, a piazza or a veranda.

Front porches, also called porticos, are attached to the front of the house and call attention to the main entrance to the home. If they have a roof, the small platforms leading up to the front door of the house, called stoops, are also considered front porches. Wraparound porches, also called verandas, extend around two or more sides of the house. Second-story porches, also called galleries, were often located off of a bedroom and used for sleeping. Open porches have no exterior walls, only pillars to support the roof. For architectural embellishment as well as safety, open porches often have a railing around the perimeter of the porch. Enclosed porches, such as three-season and screened-in styles, are popular in cooler climates or where insects are a problem.

A recent development in porches is the sun porch. These sunny spaces are popular in climates where weather prohibits year-round outdoor living. Originally designed to bring the warmth of sunlight indoors, these sunny spaces are not specifically porches or conservatories.

Traditional porches can also be considered passive solar devices. Properly designed and oriented, a porch keeps the sun away from ground-floor windows, reducing heat gain in the house. In winter, the low angle of the sun's rays allows sunlight to enter ground floor windows, providing heat gain through the greenhouse effect.

(inset above) **A simple front stoop** becomes an elegant entrance when special attention is paid to architectural design details.

(top photo) **The old-fashioned appeal** of a porch enhances and complements the basic square shape of this house.

(bottom photo) **This modern-day sun porch** expands the interior living space and brings a panoramic view of the breathtaking scenery so close you can almost touch it.

Photo courtesy of Walpole Woodworkers Inc.

# FRONT PORCHES

From a simple raised platform under a modest roof at the front entrance, to an elaborate Victorian design that spans the front of the house, front porches have the ability to transform a simple home into something special. Even if it's a small or basic porch, not used for outdoor living or extended activities, such as a front stoop, a front porch adds an interesting architectural flair to the front of a house. The traditional elegance a front porch adds often makes it the focal point of the home.

One of the most endearing qualities of porches is their ability to link your home to the outside world. Until the arrival of automobiles, with their smelly exhaust fumes and loud engines, the front porch was almost a social necessity. It served as a place to catch up on the latest gossip with the neighbors and find out what was happening in other parts of town from passersby.

*Restoring a front porch to its original beauty can be a major undertaking, but it's well worth the effort when the end result is an elegant entrance and front porch that can be enjoyed by everyone.*

Photo courtesy of Ned Skubic

*Even a modest summer cottage expands its living space with a front porch. The low garden wall makes this private space more public and promotes interaction between those on the porch and people passing by.*

**This front porch can also be considered a veranda,** *because it spans the entire front of this house. The natural texture of the brick used for the porch goes well with the texture of the stucco exterior.*

*Indoor/outdoor ceramic tile keeps this back porch cool and comfortable.*

## Design

# BACK PORCHES

Back porches are usually more private than those located in the front of a house. Back porches often connect to an interior kitchen or family room, making them conveniently located, comfortable spaces for many activities. A back porch provides a cool, comfortable place to sit and relax, a reprieve from a hot, sunny patio or a pleasant, comfortable place for a social gathering or family barbecue.

Back porches often function as utility porches, providing a handy place to drop groceries, store bicycles and garden tools or leave muddy or wet shoes, boots or umbrellas.

*(above)* **A second-story balcony** wraps around the back of this house and overlooks an active deck area below. A portion of the deck has been screened in, creating a bug-free back porch

*(left)* **Large round columns** that frame this back porch are reminiscent of a Greek temple. The absence of railings makes the porch feel more open and spacious.

*(right)* **The all-glass roof** and walls of this sun porch give new meaning to the phrase "greenhouse effect."

# WRAPAROUND PORCHES

Wraparound porches, also called verandas, extend along two, three or all four sides of a house. Originally designed to accommodate warm-weather activities, wraparound porches increase your chances of finding the most comfortable outdoor area. By giving you access to more than one side of the house, they allow you to choose sun or shade, a breeze or shelter from it, as comfort dictates.

When a porch extends around two or more sides of a house its role often changes from one side of the house to another. On one side of the house, the porch might be secluded, quiet and accessed from a bedroom—the perfect setting for a private sleeping porch. On the other side, it might extend across the front of the house, creating a pleasant and comfortable area to chat with neighbors and greet guests.

Photo courtesy of Weatherend Estate Furniture

***Outdoor dining*** *is cool and comfortable out on this back porch veranda.*

Photo courtesy of Lindal Cedar Homes Inc., Seattle, Washington

***This extensive wraparound*** *porch allows access to all sides of the house. This second-story wraparound provides a panoramic view of the wide-open spaces, as well as access to the most comfortable outdoor conditions.*

Photo courtesy of Architectural Facades Unlimited Inc.

***The grandeur and elegance of this wraparound porch*** *come from giving special attention to the details in the facade, such as the pillars, railings and balustrades. This expansive porch has more than one exposure, allowing you to take advantage of the sun, and other climate-controlling factors, as they change throughout the day.*

# OPEN PORCHES

Open porches are the living rooms of summer; they can be tucked into the corner of an L-shaped house, where they are sheltered on one side, or they can wrap around the entire house, creating separate activity areas on each side.

Open porches allow you to commune with nature, yet maintain some sense of protection or shelter. These open-air living spaces add architectural interest to a house, especially if they complement the rest of the home's exterior.

A fabric shade can be a handy addition to an open porch design. The shade provides privacy and protection and can be rolled up or down, as desired. These durable, water-repellent porch shades are made by awning companies and are available in a variety of colors and styles.

Photo courtesy of Archadeck

*(above)* **An open front porch** *helps link the private space inside the house with the public space in front. An open porch allows users to become a part of public life or maintain their privacy within the protective confines of the porch.*

*(left)* **An overhead pergola** *and a translucent screen lessen the intensity of the hot sun on this open porch.*

*(left)* **A Creole influence** can be seen in the architectural style of this open, second-story porch, located in New Orleans' French Quarter.

*(right)* **This unique porch** design features an open roof that creates an effect similar to an arbor. The shape, color and style of the roof and attached railing visually tie the entire porch area together for a unified look.

# ENCLOSED PORCHES

With the invention of air-conditioning and the popularity of the backyard patio, people began enclosing their porches and converting them for year-round use. Porches can be permanently screened in, completely enclosed by glazed windows, or convertible. A relatively new porch alternative, convertible porches can be easily converted to open, screened or glass walls for comfortable use all year round. Enclosed porches create children's play areas that are sheltered and close by for easy observation.

Screened porches are flexible alternatives to complete openness. Enclosing an open porch transforms it into a more private place. If you want to maintain maximum openness and visual uniformity, use double-glazed glass for the walls.

These indoor/outdoor spaces are effective alternatives for people with smaller houses who want to expand their living space—they close up to become interior rooms in the cold winter months and can be converted to open or screened porches for the warmer summer months.

Photo courtesy of Ro-Tile Inc.

*A **large masonry porch** looks out over a beautiful enclosed pool area. This commercial version of an enclosed sun porch lets swimmers enjoy natural sunlight in a comfortable environment regardless of the outside temperature.*

**This enclosed porch** functions as an interior room, yet the expansive glass walls dissolve the barrier between the interior and exterior spaces, creating an indoor space with an outdoor ambience.

**This contemporary conservatory** is designed for year-round living. Accessible from inside the house or from outside on the deck, this sun porch creates a link and helps ease the transition between the two spaces.

# SUN PORCHES

Sun porches and conservatories are porch spaces that reflect a more romantic era, when house and garden came together within a room of glass. By definition, sun porches are porches that receive a lot of sun. They are often all-glass structures or enclosed porches with floor-length windows and skylights.

Conservatories originated in England, where they were designed as winter growing spaces for delicate fruits and flowers. In the early 1980s, a new type of sun-room, called a sun porch, became popular around the United States. These open, glassed-in living spaces serve as a source of solar heat and can be used year-round. Sun porches can also be used for traditional porch activities, as well as for a place to garden; you can even install a hot tub inside them.

The basic concept of the sun porch evolved from the conservatory. Sun porches and conservatories bring an interior space closer to nature, creating a sense of openness without compromising comfort and protection. The way you wish to use your sun porch will help determine the location. Southern exposures are best for capturing the most daylight but may be too hot in warm climates. In cool climates, positioning a conservatory with windows that will catch the sun as it moves from east to west will enable it to collect heat throughout most of the day.

The primary framing materials used to construct a sun porch or conservatory are wood or aluminum. On the market today, there are many prefabricated kits, as well as custom designs, for these structures. The prices for standard kits can begin at $4,000 and go as high as $50,000, depending on size and detail. Additional costs can include building a foundation and installation of the kit, electrical work and flooring installation. These extras can increase the total cost by one-and-a-half to two-and-a-half times the price of the kit.

Photo courtesy of Lindal Cedar Homes Inc., Seattle, Washington

*The glass ceiling gives this contemporary sun porch the look and feel of a traditional conservatory. Operational windows can be opened or closed, as desired, to direct the flow of air through the space.*

*(right)* **A sliding glass patio door** *makes this sun porch "convertible." The door can stay closed, or it can be completely opened, eliminating the barrier between inside and out.*

*(below)* **A glassed-in sun porch** *lets you enjoy "outdoor" living all year long. The frame consists of solid mullions of Western red cedar, which give the interior of this sun porch a richer, more formal quality.*

# PATIO MATERIALS

The most important part of creating a patio is establishing a hard surface that will stay firm in all weather and won't sink or tip as the ground settles. The materials you choose should be strong enough to withstand the weight of patio furniture or a barbecue grill. Some of the most popular surfaces include paving slabs, bricks bedded into mortar or sand, poured concrete or patio tiles.

Carefully consider the aesthetic effect of the material you've chosen for your patio surface, since it will have a dramatic impact on the overall look of the entire area. For example, you can buy second-hand bricks which have an authentic aged look to them, or you can buy new bricks in a variety of styles and colors to suit a more contemporary outdoor setting.

Concrete patio slabs are popular because they're attractive, convenient to use and extremely durable. Like bricks, precast concrete pavers offer a number of options for patios. Exposed aggregate pavers have small stones embedded into the molded concrete. The aggregate gives them a nonskid surface and a rough texture that blends well with rustic outdoor surroundings.

Clay patio tiles, such as terra-cotta, are smooth, resistant to wear, and easy to clean. Patio tiles are ceramic tiles whose rigid geometric shapes give patios a gracious, formal look. Quarry tile is more expensive and is more regular in shape.

Flagstone is cut from many different types of rock, the most common being sandstone and limestone, depending on location. Slate is also considered a flagstone. Slates are usually purple or gray and are harder and more durable. Flagstones can vary in thickness to help keep the surface level. These are the most expensive surfacing material you can buy, but they give an elegant permanence when laid correctly.

Loose materials, such as wood chips or gravel, are also options for a patio surface. Wood chips are springy and easy to apply. They make a soft surface under swings and slides in children's play areas. Gravel is the cheapest, yet one of the most attractive, materials you can use for a patio. It's also the quickest and easiest to put down or move. Gravel is very adaptable and looks good in almost any setting, from a rustic garden to an ultramodern backyard. Gravel also blends nicely with other materials and drains well.

*Tile products for patios* include (clockwise from top left): shell stone tile; ceramic tile, which is frost-resistant and nonskid; ceramic tile, cut to form an ashlar bond pattern; and quarry tile.

Photo courtesy of Cy DeCosse Inc.

**This natural-looking** stone patio is actually made from colored, textured concrete that has been imprinted to give it a realistic texture.

**Natural flagstone pavers** were inset in the center of this planting area, creating a rustic-looking path and a small patio area. The light color and rough texture of the flagstone create an interesting contrast to the red brick used in the surrounding patio.

**Formal red brick** paving coordinates with the brick exterior of the house. The uniform pattern is set off by precise white grout lines.

# Design
# PATIO OPTIONS

Patios offer an effective way to increase your outdoor living space and reduce the amount of maintenance your yard requires by reducing the amount of lawn area. Patios are perfect for people who want low-maintenance landscapes for their yards. They can be any size or shape and custom-fit to almost any area. Patios can even be built around existing trees and other landmarks. Their flexibility makes patios one of the most convenient ways to enhance an outdoor living space.

Patio designs range from a simple concrete pad, accessorized with a picnic table and some potted plants, to an elaborate courtyard, complete with designer furniture, a theme garden and a pond. To be functional, a patio should be as large as a standard room—100 square feet or more. You can designate different activity areas by using a different paving material in each area. You can control the climate on your patio by incorporating a roof or a fence into the setting. An arbor over your patio will give you shade, if desired, or let the light through, if it isn't. Patios made of masonry materials such as brick, flagstone, concrete and tile, usually have an intimate quality and offer a sense of shelter and protection. Patios can be surrounded by walls or fences for privacy, as seen in the patios of old Spanish courtyards.

Patios are usually expansive spaces facing an inviting view of a garden, pool or other outdoor setting. Straight lines and right angles give a formal feel to a patio design. A patio design that uses curving lines creates a more casual-looking space. A custom-designed patio can be fit into almost any setting. Detached patios are separate from the house and are often located in far-off corners of your yard. Attached patios are connected to your house. An attached patio is best for entertaining or outdoor dining because it is close to the house and has easy access to the kitchen. Poolside and combination patios are designs that incorporate other structural features of the yard into the patio itself, as in a patio that incorporates part of a deck design.

Photo courtesy of Cy DeCosse Inc.

*An artistic patio design* combines concrete aggregate pavers with smooth concrete pavers. The different surfaces complement one another and create an interesting contrast in color and texture.

(above) **A simple brick patio** provides a comfortable place to sit and enjoy an evening outdoors. Solid cedar furniture adds a rustic charm to the natural beauty of the red brick.

(left) **Large flagstone pavers** are used to create an interesting patio effect in this small backyard space.

# ATTACHED PATIOS

Patios that attach to your home not only expand your usable living space to the outdoors, they also make your house appear larger than it actually is. Patios often can be accessed from many areas of the home. Those located just off the living room, family room and kitchen are especially effective for outdoor entertaining and dining.

Sliding glass or French patio doors help to minimize the barrier between indoors and outside with a transparent wall of glass. Arbors and trellises can be added for protection or privacy, and small planting areas, or container gardens, soften the hard edges with color.

Photo courtesy of Bomanite Corp.

*(above)* **A multilevel patio** *attaches to the house and expands the usable outdoor living space tremendously. This multifunctional patio can be accessed from many areas of the house, making dining and entertaining easier and more convenient.*

*(left)* **Large French doors** *open onto an attached formal brick patio. The comfortable patio area invites people to cross the threshold and step into the outdoor space.*

Photo courtesy of Andersen Windows Inc.

*(right)* **This Mediterranean-style** *home features an enclosed courtyard patio. A large, natural-stone fountain is the centerpiece of this elegant patio.*

*(right)* **Interlocking paving stones** *are an easy way to create a natural-looking attached patio. Rich color of the natural-looking terra-cotta contrasts beautifully with the lush green of the surrounding landscape.*

35

*(above)* **This private outdoor oasis** *was created by placing a small brick patio away from the house. Tall bushes and a short stone garden wall enclose the space, making it secluded and private.*

*(right)* **A meticulously laid brick walkway** *incorporates a herringbone brick pattern seen throughout the landscape, and connects a detached patio with the rest of the yard. The contrasting colors in the brick give the path visual texture.*

*Design*

# DETACHED PATIOS

A detached patio creates a private outdoor area, where you can get away from it all for a bit of quiet relaxation. A detached patio helps you utilize more of your yard by transforming an area of the yard that probably wouldn't get much use into usable space.

Detached patios can be built on almost any type of lot, flat or sloped, and to almost any size and shape desired. A geometrically shaped patio, such as a square or rectangle, will create a more formal-looking patio. A patio that is curved or irregularly shaped will have an informal appeal.

Decorative paths and walkways can be used effectively to connect a detached patio to other areas of the yard and integrate the elements of your landscape into one unified design. Even a simple garden path will lead followers to an intimate patio area.

*A small garden path* made of patio tiles leads to a clearing, where it widens to form a small patio area in this flower-filled garden. This tiny patio is just big enough for a small table-and-chairs set, and the perfect place for afternoon tea.

*Irregular flagstone* creates a nice walkway through a garden. A formal brick walkway encircles the garden area. The clean finished look of the brick makes a nice contrast to the rough texture of the flagstone.

*This charming patio setting uses a multilevel design, with very subtle changes in levels, to effectively define the different areas of this patio. A step up to a second level of the patio defines a formal dining area that is separated from the rest of the patio.*

## Design

# MULTILEVEL PATIOS

Large lots, or those with many changes in ground level, are perfect for multilevel patios. Areas of uneven ground beautifully accommodate a raised or sunken patio. The different levels are linked by steps or pathways.

A multilevel patio increases the flexibility of the patio area by creating separate areas that can be used for different functions or activities. Retaining walls are a common way to create a patio area with a raised lawn on one level and a sunken patio on a lower level.

*A small backyard patio handles a sloping incline by dividing the area into different levels. One side of the patio is inset into the hill by a small retaining wall. On the other side, a step down is required when going from the patio to the next activity area.*

(above) **Different surface materials,** as well as different levels, separate this backyard patio into distinctly defined activity areas.

(right) **A steep incline is tamed** by a series of brick steps, leading down from a small brick patio at the top of a hill. These steps are multilevel by design; as they descend the hill, small landing areas act as different levels. These landing areas are large enough to accommodate a small bench or a small gathering of people.

# POOLSIDE PATIOS

When a pool takes center stage in an outdoor setting, poolside patios accommodate the activities that take place around a pool. Safety is one of the primary factors to be considered with these types of patios. The materials used for the surface should be nonslip. They should also be cool and comfortable underfoot, even in the hot sun.

How formal or informal your poolside patio appears depends on the shape of the pool, and the patio that surrounds it. Rigid geometric rectangles and squares create a formal atmosphere. Irregular, curving shapes create a more natural and informal setting.

Poolside patios are often home to hot tubs. These attractive and functional features add an element of interest to the setting. Dining and eating areas, as well as food preparation areas and storage, are other elements that increase the flexibility of a poolside patio.

***Traditional brick pavers*** *are an ideal choice for a poolside patio. They are smooth and comfortable underfoot, the irregular surface makes them nonslip and the natural colors keep the surface from getting too hot under bright sunlight.*

*(right)* **Light-colored patio tiles** *and cement slabs create a poolside patio that coordinates with the white adobe exterior of the house and creates a unified look for the entire setting.*

**An elaborate poolside patio** *carries the Spanish style of the house to the patio area surrounding the pool. Red brick frames the spacious patio area and ties visually with the red clay tiles on the roof.*

# INTEGRATED PATIOS

Patios are often integrated with other landscape features such as pools, decks or retaining walls to form the perfect partnership of form, function and beauty. These integrated patio designs feature multiple levels, a mix of materials and a union of structural elements such as patio tiles with redwood decking in order to form functional and unique outdoor living areas.

More and more people are discovering that the materials used in patios and decks actually complement each other and create a striking aesthetic appeal. For example, a highly successful idea for an integrated patio setting is one that combines masonry materials with wooden decking to enhance the shape and texture of the patio and create a truly unique environment.

*This **multifaceted outdoor area** integrates a wooden deck with ceramic patio tiles and red brick pavers. The natural colors and textures of the materials complement one another beautifully.*

*A **spacious veranda** meets with a poolside patio for an interesting contrast. Textured cement re-creates the look of real patio tiles and gives the porch area an interesting look that defines it beautifully and differentiates it from the smooth surface of the cement slabs surrounding the pool.*

**A small brick patio** provides the background for this integrated outdoor setting. The multicolored bricks pick up the various colors seen throughout the landscape, such as the light brown stain used on the deck, or the dark color of the railroad ties that form the planter boxes, and help to visually unify the look.

Photos this page courtesy of Milt Charno & Associates

**The cement surface** of a poolside patio integrates easily with the wood deck and wood fence that surround the space. River rock was used in poolside planting areas to help soften the transition from the deck to the patio.

*Design*

# ACCENTS & ACCESSORIES FOR PORCHES & PATIOS

Furnishing and accessorizing a porch or patio can be as interesting and exciting as accessorizing any interior part of the house. The outdoor furniture you choose will establish the personality of an outdoor space. It should be functional, aesthetically pleasing and complement the design style of other elements.

Comfort and durability should be primary concerns when choosing outdoor furniture. Furniture that will be used outdoors must be able to withstand natural elements like heat and moisture. Most garden furniture is constructed of aluminum, wrought iron, steel or naturally resistant wood, such as teak or cedar. If you live in a damp climate, consider painted or enameled furniture, which resists rust.

Combining built-in features, such as built-in benches and planters, with movable furniture makes a porch or patio much more flexible and functional. A built-in bench can serve a number of functions, from overflow seating when you entertain, to buffet counters for outdoor suppers, or platforms for container plants.

Benches, love seats and other accessories can be tailored to fit the contours and proportions of any porch or patio. Specialty items can be used to create a theme or special atmosphere. For example: an old-fashioned porch swing adds a taste of tradition and provides comfortable seating for quiet reading or simple relaxation.

Color can be added to a porch or patio by including small planting areas or containers filled with colorful flowers. You can also create a specific theme on a porch or patio by keeping the colors and patterns consistent in the paints and fabrics used to accessorize.

**Inset planting areas** *were created by coordinating the placement of modeled cement patio tiles. The planting areas, which seem to emerge from the patio itself, help soften the hard edges of the cement with softer textures and colors.*

*The flowing lines of the built-in bench* design create a striking contrast with the formal feel of a traditional brick patio. Poured cement was used to create a light border that frames the outside edges of the different patio levels. Large boulders are scattered throughout the area, tucked among the lush green shrubs and trees.

(above) **Container gardens** are an ideal way to add color and texture to any outdoor setting. They are easy to maintain and can be brought indoors when the weather gets too cold.

(right) **A small statue** can add subtle charm to any outdoor area.

*Functional, stylish garden furniture,* like this elegant teak outdoor dining table and chairs, makes dining outdoors so pleasant that every meal is a special occasion.

Photo courtesy of Bobbie Lopatin, Country Casual

*The distinctive design* of this garden bench, matching armchair and coffee table incorporates details found in fine interior furniture. These innovative designs are practical solutions to comfortable enjoyment.

*Cast aluminum* is used to produce an outdoor dining table with a decorative top and matching chairs. Cast-aluminum furniture is beautiful, durable and comfortable.

# ACCENTS & ACCESSORIES

The latest colors, designs and materials for outdoor furniture and accessories add a festive touch to any outdoor environment. With the increasing popularity of porches and patios comes an increased interest in furniture and accessories for these outdoor areas.

The range of available outdoor accessories includes benches, chairs, tables, planter boxes, cooking areas, sun screens and large colorful umbrellas, just to name a few. These specialty furnishings and accessories range from re-creations of traditional furniture styles in metal or wicker, to contemporary new designs made of plastic or canvas. The outdoor furniture you choose should complement and coordinate with the exterior style, colors and materials of your house.

**An outdoor umbrella** *is an all-purpose accessory for any outdoor setting. This octagonal umbrella is constructed from solid teak so it won't warp or rot. The solid metal base keeps the umbrella steady and fits neatly under a table.*

**Inexpensive outdoor furniture** *doesn't have to look cheap. This white aluminum table and chair set give this small patio a formal feel and bring a splash of crisp color to the background of red brick.*

# ACCENTS & ACCESSORIES

Fire pits and barbecues are multifunctional accents that are common additions to an outdoor setting. They not only offer a source of heat, they also double as seats or tables when not being used as a heat source.

If cooling off is one of the functions of your outdoor space, the refreshing sensation of water will be a welcome addition to your outdoor environment. Even though a pond or water garden can't be part of the porch itself, the allure of these interesting elements can certainly be enjoyed from a front or back porch. Pools, ponds, fountains and water gardens are often included in patios and other outdoor areas for functional as well as aesthetic reasons. Besides bringing its reflective beauty to a setting, water also adds moisture to the air and an element of soothing coolness the hot, sunny patio.

*Photo courtesy of Architectural Facades Unlimited Inc.*

***This fabulous fountain*** *is an elegant addition to this formal patio. Small shrubs are tucked around the base of the fountain, and wide, flat edges at the top of the base offer ample seating for those who want to dabble in the water directly.*

*This formal English garden* brings the appreciation of artistic beauty outdoors. A small statue is prominently displayed, with plenty of seating surrounding it for those who wish to sit and soak up the scenery.

*An outdoor fire pit* is a fun and functional accessory for any outdoor area. The brick construction blends with the rest of the patio, while the smooth, round shape adds an element of interest and shape to an otherwise bare space.

# PORCH
# &
# PATIO
# IDEAS

# ENTRY PORCHES & PATIOS

There is no denying the warm, welcoming effect of entry porches or patios. Traditional front porches have always conjured up friendly images of summer days and lemonade, while more modern front sun porches help to disperse sunlight throughout the building and change the entire appearance of the home. It's important to personalize these structures so that they blend with your needs and the architectural design of the home. The porch featured above, for example, seems vaguely Old World with its dark, overhead construction and patterned railings.

While front porches were once one of the most popular features of a home, today many front porches have taken a back seat to their backyard counterparts. An entry patio gives the home an original look and feel, and takes full advantage of yard space that might otherwise be wasted.

Your options are just as plentiful in the front yard as they are in the back. From a raised platform to a sunny covered porch, entry porches and patios can transform your yard and home and help you get the most from your available space.

Entry porches and patios don't always have to sacrifice privacy. You can take steps to make them just as hidden and private as any backyard grotto. High walls, thick shrubs and creative landscaping ideas do wonders to keep areas personal. One advantage of entry porches and patios, however, is that they can be as private or public as you want.

*A great bank of windows* helps funnel fresh sunlight into this impressive porch and throughout the home. Obviously, this entry porch adds a whole new element to the appearance of this traditional structure.

***The first-floor doors*** *serve double duty as windows on this multifunction porch. The two levels take advantage of the available space, while the support columns give the entire scene a grand, almost royal, appearance.*

(right) **An entry patio** in the true sense of the word; the walls and vegetation are fully utilized to show just how private an entry can be.

(right) **Sometimes a small patio** can be a purely decorative item. A simple stairway would do little to flatter this entry.

Photo courtesy of Ned Skubic

*(above)* **A traditional entry porch** *can be a truly impressive sight. This columned giant announces the home with authority and grace.*

Photo courtesy of Awning Division of the Industrial Fabrics Assn. Intl.

*(right)* **Modern entries,** *though less imposing than those of years past, often blend into the house structure, making one seem like an extension of the other.*

*(left)* **This Spanish-style** *entry features both a porch and patio. They blend perfectly with the home while providing needed privacy and shelter.*

*(above)* **This quaint old-style porch** *is perfect for afternoons of relaxation and conversation.*

*(right)* **A narrow, tiled porch precedes** *the front door, creating a friendly, welcoming atmosphere.*

Photo courtesy of Lindal Cedar Homes Inc., Seattle, Washington

*(right)* **This simple porch** *matches the house perfectly and gives the family space to enjoy their rural surroundings.*

Photo courtesy of Ned Skubic

*(right)* **This small porch** *provides much-needed contrast to the plain appearance of the house entry.*

*Two simple doors* flood the entire room with fresh sunlight. Patio entrances help to bring the outdoors inside while maintaining the atmosphere of an outdoor living room.

# QUIET & PRIVATE PORCHES & PATIOS

The best porches and patios take advantage of quiet, private areas without seeming oppressive or confining. Take advantage of your space and landscape resources to create the porch or patio that best fits your lifestyle.

Porches and patios don't need to be situated in heavy woods to shelter you from noise and distractions. With additional walls, fences and shrubbery, even urban settings can become quiet, private places in which to seek solace. With the right combination of landscaping and structural elements, your porch or patio can seem like an indoor room with a direct link to the outdoors.

How a porch or patio is situated around a house is very important for privacy. A raised platform or a second-story porch automatically ensures a certain level of seclusion. Many people place a porch or patio in the corner formed by an L-shaped house. In this way, the home itself provides a great deal of privacy. For even more enclosure, consider an overhead structure, such as a vine-covered arbor.

It's important to remember that patios and porches are, by definition, outdoor-related features. Some privacy must be sacrificed to enjoy the expanse of nature. Whether you're considering an enclosed sun porch on the front of your home, or a simple concrete patio in the backyard, try to strike the perfect balance between outdoor freedom and personal comfort.

Photo courtesy of Cy DeCosse Inc.

*Nature provides a feeling of seclusion* in this open-air patio, proving that detached patios can be quiet and private with the right combination of landscaping and design.

*(left)* **The owners of this enclosed porch** *truly know what it means to bring the outdoors into the home. This cozy seating area might as well be the family living room.*

*(below)* **For increased privacy,** *you might want to consider an arbor or some other form of overhead construction. An arbor serves many functions, such as blocking noise, the sun and outside disturbances.*

Photo courtesy of Walpole Woodworkers Inc.

Photo courtesy of Bobbie Lopatin, Country Casual

*(above)* **It's generally easier to find privacy** in the backyard. This porch allows the family to watch the children at play while enjoying the outdoors under the shade of a solid roof.

*(left)* **Even an open-air porch can** offer intimate surroundings with the right furniture and accessories.

*(above)* **A wooden wall ensures a level of privacy;** and it doesn't need to be obtrusive. Cover the interior walls with crawling vines or large shrubs to soften their surfaces.

*(left)* **Even the suggestion** of overhead construction lends the feel of privacy to a scene. It's important to keep the construction consistent with the style of the home.

65

*A **raised wooden deck** serves as a roof to this space-saving combination porch/patio. The trees and shrubs along the borders practically enclose the area to form a private outdoor room.*

*(above)* **An interior sun porch** *ensures complete privacy. The windows allow complete visual exposure to the outdoors while providing a secure, indoor setting.*

*(right)* **This scenic overlook** *was a private spot long before it became a backyard patio. A comfortable bench is all that's needed to complete a tranquil scene.*

Photo courtesy of Sticks and Stones Innovative Decks & Landscape Design

*(left)* **This modern, second-story patio** *seems at home among the trees and is all but obscured by the surrounding foliage.*

Photo courtesy of Lindal Cedar Homes Inc., Seattle, Washington

*(above)* **An open-air porch** *is raised and semienclosed for a certain measure of privacy. More important, however, is its wide-open feel, which overlooks a stunning view of the lake.*

**A *wraparound porch*** usually adds up to at least one private area. This backyard structure is shielded from prying eyes and ears in part by the house construction, which includes several access doors to the porch.

Photo courtesy of Andersen Windows Inc.

*(right)*
**A sun porch**
*combines the
freedom of the
outdoors with the
privacy and shelter
of a living room.*

Photo courtesy of Lindal Cedar Homes Inc., Seattle, Washington

*(above)* **The overhead**
*windows provide an open-air touch to
this backyard porch, which meshes perfectly with
the architectural style of the home.*

Photo courtesy of Metropolitan Ceramics Inc.

**This porch opens up to all outdoors,** *while the home's interior is flooded with light from a bank of large glass doors. In this way, the family can experience the privacy of their home while enjoying the beauty of the scenery.*

*(above)* **A colorful awning** *provides a decorative touch to this contemporary backyard porch, showing a true partnership of privacy and style.*

*(above right)* **Multilevel patios** *allow you to create private areas for any number of activities. This circular platform is located away from the main patio area. It combines with some attractive outdoor furniture to create a secluded dining area.*

*(right)* **Having the right accessories** *can make all the difference on a porch or patio. When you need shade or privacy, for instance, a portable umbrella can do the work of an overhang or awning without the feeling of enclosure.*

*A background courtyard* is given a bit more style and privacy with the overhead construction. This overhead design keeps the area light and sunny while maintaining a solid rooflike appearance.

**This secluded platform** is located far away from the hustle and bustle of the city. It combines a beautiful view with some attractive outdoor furniture to create a spectacular dining area.

*(left)* **Positioning the patio** *away from the home gives the area a more secluded feel.*

**Small conversational areas** *are made more intimate with the right amount of vegetation, which acts as a kind of shelter for this patio grotto.*

*(right)* **When all else fails,** *a solid wall does wonders for a private patio. An overhead structure by the door and a decorative flower garden help to soften the atmosphere.*

*(above)* **Sun porches are becoming** *a much more common means to enjoy the outdoors in the security of your home. Location is the key, however. In some areas, too much direct sunlight can make a sun porch too hot to enjoy.*

# DINING & ENTERTAINING ON PORCHES & PATIOS

Outdoor settings can be ideal for home entertainment and dining. A gathering of friends and loved ones among the sights, sounds and scents of the outdoors has a profound and lasting effect. Each activity is different, however, and you should understand just what your needs will be before planning a porch or patio. For large parties, it's hard to beat a multilevel patio. A large, well-lit backyard with a creative patio or porch and an interesting landscape can be a source of entertainment in itself. Of course, in an outdoor setting, cleanup is easy, and the risk of damage is small. In areas where biting insects are a problem, a screened porch is almost a necessity.

Relaxing meals outside are an integral part of having a porch or patio. Many people incorporate grills into the scene to create a functional combination of kitchen, dining room and family room in one.

One of the outstanding aspects of dining and entertaining on a porch or patio is that the entire family can enjoy the experience to the fullest. Children can play or eat without worrying about making a mess, and adults can relax in the knowledge that there's nothing outside for their children to destroy. Even better, many porches and patios are elevated, allowing parents to keep a watchful eye on their children at play.

Entertaining or dining on these outdoor features need not be affected by size constraints. In the right design or setting, a small porch is just as enjoyable as a sprawling wraparound. Gauge your needs against your desires, and get ready to enjoy the great outdoors.

*The classic columns* and hardwood floors on this traditional front porch give the dining area a formal, almost royal appearance.

(both photos) **Dining and entertaining** *is most enjoyable when you are in contact with nature. Whether you're having a polite, formal party or an outdoor bash, a porch or patio can help to focus the fun and make the scene more relaxing. Comfortable outdoor furniture makes the patio at right a more pleasant place to sit and enjoy the sunshine, while the multilevel porch below is perfect for an outdoor party or reception.*

Photo courtesy of Sticks and Stones Innovative Decks & Landscape Design

(below) **This combination patio/deck** *makes the whole area more enjoyable. If it's done well, the transition between deck and patio will be subtle and smooth.*

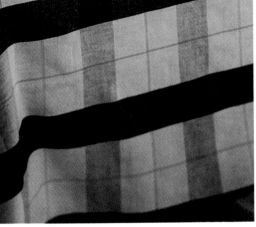

(above) **Special decorative lanterns** *add charm to the dinner. Just as in the dining room, small touches like these can transform the scene.*

(right) **With the sun setting** *in the background, this indoor sun porch makes dinnertime a pleasure.*

Photo courtesy of Lindal Cedar Homes Inc., Seattle, Washington

*(above)* **You may not need an elaborate porch or patio.** *This simple backyard patio is perfect for sipping lemonade or enjoying a cookout. For privacy and shade, a trellis borders one side of the patio.*

*(above)* **A simple dining set blends** *perfectly with the large stones of this courtyard patio.*

*(left)* **A built-in windbreak** *provides shelter and makes cooking in the fire pit an easy task.*

# PORCHES & PATIOS FOR RECREATION

As free time becomes harder and harder to come by in our busy world, more and more people are looking to create convenient sources of recreational space at home. Porches and patios are two of the most logical resources.

When discussing patio recreation, a common subject is water. Pools and hot tubs are ideal for patio fun, and many homeowners choose to incorporate one or both into their patio scheme. From the patio you can relax in the sun or watch as your friends and family play games in the pool. The fun needn't stop at sundown; good lighting and a hot tub allow you to enjoy the patio day or night.

Sunny patios are often favorite spots for hobbyists. Painters, in particular, find the brightness of patios conducive to their creative process. Many people place exercise machines on an enclosed porch or patio to add scenery to what can be a boring indoor routine.

Whether on a porch or a patio, your recreational options are nearly boundless. If you like gardening, these features help to make the plants seem a little closer. If outdoor sports are more your style, they give you convenient access to the backyard's open spaces. Whatever your choice, design and build the porch or patio to make the most of your valuable time.

*(above)* **This sprawling pool deck** *is perfect for the Spanish-style home in the backround. Overlooking the scene is a raised patio, which has easy access to the home and provides a keen vantage point on the pool below.*

*(above)* **Multiple levels** *allow you to customize your recreational space to make the most of your patio or porch.*

*(left)* **This indoor sun porch takes** *advantage of natural light and heat and even includes a relaxing whirlpool for hours of fun and enjoyment.*

*(above)* **A backyard patio** *gives you plenty of options. Here we see an elegant brick patio with bordering flower gardens and a pool. Such a patio design utilizes wide-open spaces in the backyard and is ideal for home recreation.*

*(right)* **This magnificent sun porch** incorporates an indoor pool to make swimming a year-round activity. The room's positioning is well chosen—notice the spectacular view in the background.

*(above)* **Sun porches are often favorite spots** for painting. The warm glow of natural light aids in the process and makes the surroundings pleasant for long hours of concentration, while the indoor setting protects the artist from wind or rain.

*(above)* **This versatile porch** *is great for sunbathing, entertaining or dining. Easy access to the pool makes it a true recreational deck, but the columns and roof are reminiscent of older, more traditional porches.*

**This beautiful garden patio** is a decorative feature of the garden itself. A patio makes it easier to enjoy a gardener's handiwork, and solid benches make entertaining easier and the entire area more versatile.

(above) **This whirlpool** is built right into the patio for easy access. Built-in pools often look more unified with the patio environment than freestanding pools.

(right) **The central feature of this small patio** is the whirlpool, which is positioned in a private backyard nook.

Photo courtesy of Jacuzzi Whirlpool Bath

93

(*above*) **What better place for a tea party** than outside on the porch? An underrated aspect of many porches and patios—they make great contained play areas for small children.

**Select the area that best fits your needs,** *then modify it to make your recreation time most enjoyable. Here, sculpture and landscaping ideas create a perfect whirlpool grotto.*

# LIST OF CONTRIBUTORS

We'd like to thank the following companies for providing the photographs used in this book:

Archadeck
U.S. Structures, Inc.
2112 West Laburnum Avenue
Richmond, VA 23227
(800) 722-4668

Architectural Facades Unlimited Inc.
1990 Stone Avenue
San Jose, CA 95125
(408) 298-2758

Andersen Windows Inc.
Bayport, MN 55003
(800) 426-4261 ext. 1503

Awning Division of the Industrial
Fabrics Association International
345 Cedar Street, Suite 800
St. Paul, MN 55101
(612) 222-2508

Bachman's Landscaping Service
6010 Lyndale Avenue South
Minneapolis, MN 55419
(612) 861-7600

Bomanite Corp.
P.O. Box 599
Madera, CA 93639
(800) 854-2094

California Redwood Association
405 Enfrente Drive, Suite 200
Novato, CA 94949
(415) 382-0662

Champlain Stone, Ltd.
P.O. Box 650
Warrensburg, NY 12885
(518) 623-2902
fax (518) 623-3088

Country Casual Garden Furnishings
17317 Germantown Road
Germantown, MD 20874
Send $3 for a 72 pg. full color catalogue of
teak garden furniture.

Durasol Awnings
Durasol Systems Inc.
197 Stone Castle Road
Rock Tavern, NY 12575
(718) 937-7632

Florentine Craftsmen, Inc.
46-24 28th Street
Long Island City, NY 11101
(718) 937-7632

Geebro Ltd.
2145 Barrett Park Drive, Suite 107
Kennesaw, GA 30144
(404) 419-7343

Jacuzzi Whirlpool Bath
Pacific Group International
2121 North California Boulevard, #690
Walnut Creek, CA 94596
(510) 472-8383

Kingsley-Bate Ltd.
5587-B Guinea Road
Fairfax, VA 22032
(703) 978-7200

Landshapes, Inc.
8016 Pleasant Avenue South
Bloomington, MN 55420
(612) 888-3771

Lindal Cedar Homes, Inc.
P.O. Box 24426
Seattle, WA 98124
(206) 725-0900

Marvin Windows & Doors
P.O. Box 100
Warroad, MN 56763
(800) 346-5128

Metropolitan Ceramics Inc.
Div. of Metropolitan Industries Inc.
P.O. Box 9240
Canton, OH 44711
(216) 484-4887

Milt Charno & Associates
611 North Mayfair Road
Wauwatosa, WI 53226
(414) 475-1965

Minneapolis Public Library
300 Nicollet Mall
Minneapolis, MN 55401-1992
(612) 372-6500

Pacific Clay Brick Products
14741 Lake Street
Lake Elsinore, CA 92530-1609
(909) 674-2131

Peachtree Doors & Windows
4350 Peachtree Ind. Blvd.
Norcross, GA 30071
(800) 477-6544

Ro-Tile Inc.
P.O. Box 410
Lodi, CA 95241
(800) 688-1380

Ned Skubic
Sundial Apt. #1
1635 NE Fourth Place
Ft. Lauderdale, FL 33301
(305) 463-7645

Silver Bullet Inc. Design & Build
2611 South First Avenue
Minneapolis, MN 55408
(612) 874-7748

Sticks and Stones Innovative Decks
and Landscape Design
2822 West 43rd Street
Minneapolis, MN 55410
(612) 920-2400

TCT Landscaping
P.O. Box 1218
Solvang, CA 93464
(805) 688-3741

Vegetable Factory Inc.
495 Post Road East
Westport, CT 06880-4433
(203) 454-0040

VELUX Roof Windows & Skylights
P.O. Box 5001
450 Old Brickyard Road
Greenwood, SC 29648
(800) 888-3589

Walpole Woodworkers Inc.
767 East Street
Walpole, MA 02081
(800) 343-6948

Wausau Tile, Inc.
P.O. Box 1520
Wausau, WI 54402-1520
(800) 388-8728

Weatherend Estate Furniture
6 Gordon Drive
Rockland, ME 04841
(207) 596-6483